DATE DUE		

Health Zone

Eat Right!

How YOU Can MAKE GOOD FOOD CHOICES

Matt Doeden

illustrations by Jack Desrocher

Consultant: Sonja Green, MD

Lerner Publications Company
Minneapolis

All characters in this book are fictional and are not based on actual persons. The characters' stories are not based on actual events. Any similarities thereof are purely coincidental.

612.3
DOE
cil
2009
22 95

Lerner Publications Company
A division of Lerner Publishing Group, Inc.
241 First Avenue North
Minneapolis, MN 55401 U.S.A.

Website address: www.lernerbooks.com

Library of Congress Cataloging-in-Publication Data

Doeden, Matt.
  Eat right! : how you can make good food choices / by Matt Doeden ;
illustrated by Jack Desrocher ; Consultant: Sonja Green.
    p. cm. — (Health Zone)
  Includes bibliographical references and index.
  ISBN 978–0–8225–7552–8 (lib. bdg. : alk. paper)
  1. Nutrition—Juvenile literature. I. Desrocher, Jack. II. Green, Sonja. III. Title.
TX355.D635 2009
612.3—dc22   2007043322

Manufactured in the United States of America
2 3 4 5 6 7 — BP — 14 13 12 11 10 09

Table of Contents

It was a *beautiful* day at the BEACH.

Tom, Megan, and a group of their friends were enjoying the sun and the ocean breeze. When a game of beach volleyball started up, they were among the first on the court.

Their first game was long and tiring. As the game was close to ending, Tom was feeling light-headed. He wasn't running as hard.

Then a player on the other team hit a serve to the corner of the court. The ball headed toward Tom. But he could only watch it fall to the sand. He didn't have the energy to go after it.

"I need a break,"
he shouted as he walked off the court.

Megan followed him. She asked if he was OK.

"I just need a snack," Tom answered. "I'm dragging a little."

"I could use some food too," Megan said. They sat down on their blanket. Tom reached into his cooler and pulled out a bottle of root beer and a bag of chips. Megan, meanwhile, grabbed some water and an apple. She watched her friend stuffing chips into his mouth and frowned.

*"You know, Tom, maybe if you ate better,
you wouldn't get tired so quickly."*

*"I don't think eating an apple
would make a difference," Tom replied.*

"You're right. But what if you ate healthy for a
whole week? I'll bet when we come back here,
you'd have twice the energy. You eat chips and
burgers every day. And you drink soda with every meal.
Why not try it my way, just to see if it works?"

Tom smiled. "Sure thing. What do I have to lose?"

Tom started his new diet that night. Instead of a burger,
he had a turkey sandwich and some grapes. For the whole
week, Megan helped him find healthful meals.

The next weekend, they headed back to the beach and
found another volleyball game. Tom started out playing
great, just as he had the week before. He spiked home
a key point. Tom's energy level stayed high as the game
dragged on. When it all came down to one point, he hit a
perfect pass to Megan. She spiked the ball over the net.
Game over!

Laughing, Megan headed to their blanket for a rest. "You
coming?" she shouted to Tom.

"No, you go ahead. I'm going to play another
game," he answered. "But while you're over there,
don't touch my orange juice!"

Chapter 1

WHAT IS Nutrition?

NUTRITION is all about the foods you take in.

It's about the food sources your body needs to be healthy. It's also about how your body uses foods.

Good nutrition is about eating healthful snacks and balanced meals. It's about making good choices when it comes to your diet.

Your body is kind of like a machine. It runs best if you give it the right kind of fuel. Cookies, candy bars, and soda might taste good. But they're not the best way to build a healthy body. Your body needs nutrients (healthful substances found in food) to operate at its best. An old expression says, *"You are what you eat."* And it's true! Healthful foods make a healthy body. Foods with lots of sugar, salt, and dangerous fats make an overweight, unhealthy body.

A lot of people think of a diet as a way to lose weight. But your diet is really just the combination of all the foods you eat. Certain diets *are* designed to help people shed pounds. But if you're eating right and getting exercise, you should never have to worry about a special weight-loss diet. **Keeping a healthful weight is really part of living a healthful, balanced lifestyle.** *It's all about the choices you make.*

A Food Guide

The U.S. Department of Agriculture (USDA) developed a food guide to help people with their diets and food choices. This guide is called MyPyramid.

MyPyramid splits foods into five main groups. The groups are grains, vegetables, fruits, milk, and meat and beans. (Oils are also a part of our diet.) You need to eat foods from each of the groups. Each food group plays an important role in helping you look and feel your best.

Grains

According to MyPyramid, grains should be a central part of most diets. Grains give us lots of energy. Good sources of grains are breads, rice, cereal, and pasta. You should try to eat mainly whole-grain foods. They have nutrients that keep you healthy. Most young people need about 6 ounces (170 grams) of grains each day. How much grain is that? Think two slices of bread and 2 cups of brown rice. Or ten whole-wheat crackers and two flour tortillas.

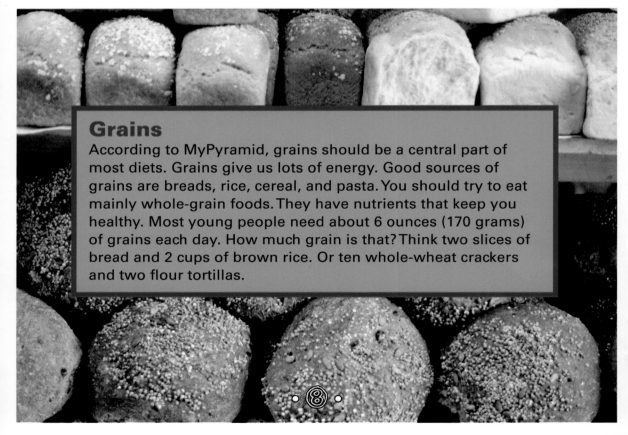

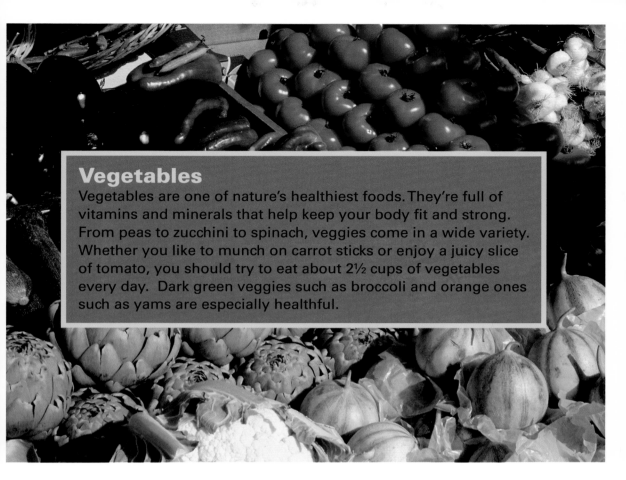

Vegetables

Vegetables are one of nature's healthiest foods. They're full of vitamins and minerals that help keep your body fit and strong. From peas to zucchini to spinach, veggies come in a wide variety. Whether you like to munch on carrot sticks or enjoy a juicy slice of tomato, you should try to eat about 2½ cups of vegetables every day. Dark green veggies such as broccoli and orange ones such as yams are especially healthful.

Fruits

Fruits are great with meals. They make even better snacks. Crisp red apples, fresh oranges, and bananas have loads of nutritional value. They're rich in nutrients like fiber and vitamin C. Most kids need about 1½ cups of fruit each day. If you can't get fresh fruit, canned and dried fruits are good options. A box of raisins fits easily into your pocket for munching on anytime.

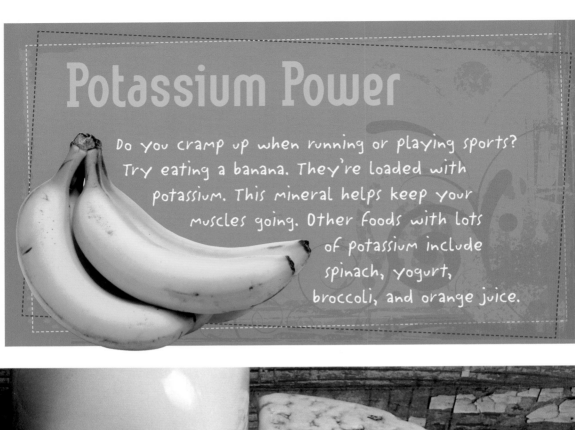

Potassium Power

Do you cramp up when running or playing sports? Try eating a banana. They're loaded with potassium. This mineral helps keep your muscles going. Other foods with lots of potassium include spinach, yogurt, broccoli, and orange juice.

Milk

The milk group includes all dairy foods (foods made from milk). Cheese, milk, and yogurt are part of the milk group. These foods are important for growing bodies. Your bones need calcium to grow strong. And the milk group is the best way to get it. It's best to look for low-fat or fat-free dairy products. Most kids need to eat about 3 cups of dairy foods each day. Kids under nine need only two cups.

Meat and Beans

Your body needs protein from meats and beans. Protein helps build bones and muscles. Beef, chicken, pork, and fish are just a few of many meat choices. Lean meats are the most healthful. A grilled chicken breast is one of the best meat choices you can make. Beans and nuts can also give your body protein. They're especially important for vegetarians (people who don't eat meat). You should eat about 5 ounces (141 g) of foods from the meat and beans group every day. If you ate one-half of a chicken breast and a couple handfuls of almonds, you'd get the 5 ounces you need.

Oils

You need some oils to keep your body healthy. Oils are not a food group. But they are an important part of a good diet. Oils can be found in nuts and fish. Vegetable oils are very healthful. Olive oil, canola oil, and soybean oil are all vegetable oils.

Eating Bugs?

In some cultures, insects are a popular food. It may sound gross. But insects can actually be a nutritious food choice. They're packed with protein and have almost no dangerous fats!

Eating Well

Everyone needs to eat a balanced diet. It's important to make sure you're getting enough food from each of the five food groups. But it can be hard to eat healthfully. Temptations come from all over. Many fast-food restaurants offer few nutritious options. Grilled chicken salads or sandwiches are good choices. But burgers and fries filled with dangerous fats can often look and smell so good. **It's OK to have that sort of meal once in a while. But it shouldn't be an everyday thing.** If you eat out a lot, learn to make healthful choices. These can include salads and specially ordered sandwiches. *Usually, if you really want to, you can find a healthful meal.*

There are some easy ways to eat more healthfully.

You can eat grilled food instead of fried snacks. You can eat whole-grain breads instead of white breads. You can reach for an apple instead of a candy bar. And one of the simplest ways to improve your diet is to cut down on soda. Regular soda is filled with sugar. It's also loaded with calories. (A calorie is a measurement of the amount of energy a certain food gives you.) Your body has to burn off these calories. But it gets little benefit from them. Diet soda isn't a great choice either. It doesn't have any calories. But it can cause dental problems. And it gives some people stomachaches. A glass of milk or water is a far better option.

Another important way to improve eating habits is by eating a balanced breakfast. Experts often call breakfast the most important meal of the day. If you start your day off right, you're less likely to overeat throughout the rest of the day. Often, people who are trying to lose weight skip breakfast as a way to cut calories. But usually, they're doing more harm than good. They only end up eating more later in the day.

Going Organic

Many people eat only organic foods. These are foods that have been grown or raised without using chemicals such as pesticides. Organic foods usually cost a little more. But lots of people think they're worth it.

Chapter 2

WHAT'S IN YOUR
Food?

A lot of people think only about the number of calories in a food.

But that tells only part of the story.

The nutrition facts panel on a package of food contains lots of other important information. Knowing how to use it can give you a head start on taking control of your diet.

On a nutrition facts panel, you'll see words like fat, carbohydrates, and protein. To understand what these and other terms mean, it's helpful to understand what your body needs. Put simply, your body needs six basic groups of nutrients. They are:

carbohydrates

fats

proteins

vitamins

minerals

water

The nutrition facts panel gives you information on all of these nutrients—except water. (Water is included in the ingredients list for foods that contain it.) **Let's take a look at these nutrients. Then you'll know why they're important in a healthful diet.**

Carbohydrates

Carbohydrates are often called carbs for short. They're a nutrient found in sugars and starches. They're common in plant products, such as fruits, vegetables, and grains. According to the MyPyramid guide, carbs should make up the biggest part of your diet. They're responsible for more than half the calories you take in.

Carbs can be divided into two groups—complex and simple. Your diet should include mostly complex carbs. The body takes a long time to digest, or break down, complex carbs. This means they provide the body with energy for a long period of time. Whole grains are a good source of complex carbs.

Simple carbs, on the other hand, are digested fairly quickly. Simple carbs are made mostly of sugars. **If you drink a soda or eat a sugar cookie, you're taking in lots of simple carbs. Simple carbs will give your body a quick burst of energy. *But it won't last*. Often in less than an hour, you'll be more tired and hungry than you were before.**

In recent years, low-carb diets have been a fad. Some people go on these diets to reduce the tired, hungry feeling that comes from eating simple carbs. They hope to control hunger with these diets. Many doctors think low-carb diets are a bad idea. Instead, they recommend eating a variety of healthful foods.

Dietary fiber is another nutrient sometimes grouped with carbs. Fiber is material that your body can't digest. But that doesn't mean that you don't need it. In fact, fiber plays a big role in your digestion. It helps keep everything moving through your system. Fiber also does a good job of filling you up. It satisfies your hunger for a longer time than other foods. Fiber cuts the risk of colon cancer too. (The colon is part of the large intestine.)

Glucose

The body breaks carbs down into a sugar called glucose. Your body uses glucose for energy. If you've ever had a sudden muscle cramp, it may have been because the muscle ran out of glucose. Runners often eat lots of complex carbs before a race. This boosts energy levels and may help cut down on muscle cramps.

fats

To many, the word *fat* is a bad thing. But fat is an important part of any diet. Some essential vitamins are fat soluble. That means that these vitamins dissolve in fat. If you don't get any fat in your diet, you're missing these key vitamins as well.

What's important is that you get the right kinds of fat—and in the right amounts. There are two basic groups of fats: **saturated** and **unsaturated**. **Saturated fats are the ones that can cause health problems.** They're linked to obesity (a condition in which a person's body carries a large amount of fat). They're also linked to heart disease. Saturated fats come mainly from animal products. Most hamburger, for example, is filled with saturated fat. Other foods heavy in saturated fats are butter, whole milk, and ice cream.

Unsaturated fats are more healthful. These fats are found in some animal products, such as fish. But they're most common in plant products. Olive oil, nuts, and soybeans are all good sources of unsaturated fats.

But not all unsaturated fats are created equal. In recent years, concern about trans fats has grown. Trans fats are artificial fats. They're sometimes used in margarine and potato chips. Trans fats are unsaturated—but they may be even worse for you than saturated fats. For years, people have been using margarine instead of butter because they thought it was more healthful. These days, many doctors are telling their patients to cut back on saturated fats but to avoid trans fats entirely.

Cholesterol

You may have heard a lot about cholesterol. Cholesterol is a waxy substance found in animal tissues and cells. There is good cholesterol and bad cholesterol. Good cholesterol is called HDL (high-density lipoprotein). Bad cholesterol is called LDL (low-density lipoprotein). High levels of LDL can lead to heart disease.

The foods you eat affect your cholesterol levels. A healthful diet raises your HDL levels. It causes your LDL levels to drop. The following chart shows how different fats affect your cholesterol levels:

Type of Fat	HDL	LDL
unsaturated	raises	lowers
saturated	lowers	raises
trans	lowers	raises

Proteins

High-protein diets are popular among bodybuilders. Protein plays a big role in muscle building. Proteins are made of amino acids. Amino acids are the building blocks of life. All cells—including muscle cells—need them to grow.

Proteins come mainly from **meat**. Every kind of meat is packed with protein. But you can also get protein from **beans**, **nuts**, and **plant products**. **Eggs** are another great source of protein. It's best to seek out sources of protein that don't have a lot of saturated fat. **Chicken** and **fish** are perfect examples.

Go NUTS

Nuts are one of nature's perfect foods. They've got plenty of protein and unsaturated fats. A snack of unsalted or lightly salted nuts is great for your energy level. It also helps your heart.

Vitamins and Minerals

Vitamins and minerals are often grouped together. They're both nutrients that the body needs. For example, your body needs vitamin B_2—found in milk, eggs, and meats—to help break down food. Vitamin C—found in citrus fruits—boosts your immune system. This helps you fight off disease. Each vitamin has its own purpose. If you're not getting enough, your body will let you know.

Minerals are just as important as vitamins. Iron is one key mineral. It's found in meats, fish, and leafy greens. Iron helps move oxygen from your blood to your cells. Calcium is another important mineral. Calcium is found in dairy foods. It helps build strong bones.

Multivitamins

Many people take daily multivitamins to make sure they're getting enough vitamins and minerals. There are different kinds of vitamin pills for men, women, and kids. If you take one, be sure it's the right kind for you. But remember: the best way to get your vitamins and minerals isn't by taking a vitamin pill. It's by eating a healthful diet.

Water

You may not think of water as a nutrient. *But it may be the most important nutrient of all.* Your body can go weeks without food. Without water, you wouldn't last more than a few days.

The body is made up of mostly water. It's in your blood and your organs. In fact, it's in every one of your body's cells. You need a constant supply of fresh water to keep everything working.

Dehydration happens when the body doesn't get enough water. A dehydrated person has headaches, a dry mouth, and weakness. If the body doesn't get fresh water, it begins to shut down. First, the kidneys fail. Other organs soon follow. One way to tell if your body has enough water is by looking at the color of your urine. If your urine is light colored, your body has enough water. If your urine is a dark yellow, you're starting to become dehydrated.

It's easy to forget about water in your diet. But drinking water is a key to having good nutrition.

Digestion

What does your body do with the foods you eat?
How does it turn a sandwich or an apple into energy?

Knowing how your body breaks down food can help you make good choices in your diet.

As soon as you start chewing your food, your body is already starting to break it down. Your teeth start to mash it up. Enzymes in your saliva begin to dissolve it. (Enzymes are digestive chemicals.) But most digestion happens in the stomach and the intestines. This is where food turns into energy.

In the stomach, your food mixes with digestive juices. These juices are rich in enzymes and acids. They break down your food into a sort of fluid. This fluid then enters your small intestine. There, more digestive juices continue the process. The food gets broken down into basic parts. Your blood absorbs these parts. It carries them throughout your entire body.

The material that doesn't get absorbed by your blood moves on to your large intestine. There, your body draws most of the water out. What's left is called feces. It's the waste material that your body didn't use.

If you've ever had diarrhea, it was because your large intestine wasn't getting the water out of your feces properly.

Breaking It Down

Your body breaks down different nutrients in different ways. It breaks most carbohydrates into glucose. Glucose is also known as blood sugar.

Your body handles fats in another way. An enzyme called lipase breaks them down into two parts: fatty acids and glycerol. It then puts them back together to form a chemical called a triglyceride. Your blood can absorb triglycerides. Once they're in your blood stream, you either have to burn them with physical activity or your body will store them as fat.

Your body gets different amounts of energy from different nutrients. Each gram of carbohydrates and proteins you eat gives you about four calories. But each gram of fat gives you about nine.

Chapter 3

Watching WHAT YOU EAT

Now that you know all about nutritients, *let's take a look at a nutrition facts panel.*

You can follow along with the example provided.
Or you can find your own examples from out of your kitchen.
Learning to read nutrition facts panels can help you watch what you eat. It's a great step toward making smarter food choices.

The Basics

The most basic information on a nutrition facts panel appears at the top. The first thing listed is serving size. This number is important. All the other numbers depend on it. If you eat more than the amount that's listed next to "serving size," the rest of the numbers will go up.

Underneath the serving size is another helpful number. It tells you how many servings are in a container. This number lets you see the total amount of servings in your package of food. You may assume certain packages contain just one serving. But check out the nutrition facts panel to be sure.

Next comes the number that many people look at first—calories. Many labels also list the number of calories that come from fat. That's an easy way to track how much fat you're getting.

Nutrition Facts

Serving Size 1 cup (30g)
Servings Per Container 17

Amount Per Serving	Wheaties	with 1/2 cup skim milk
Calories	110	150
Calories from Fat	10	10

	% Daily Value**	
Total Fat 1g*	**1%**	**2%**
Saturated Fat 0g	**0%**	**0%**
Trans Fat 0g		
Polyunsaturated Fat 0g		
Monounsaturated Fat 0g		
Cholesterol 0mg	**0%**	**1%**
Sodium 210mg	**9%**	**11%**
Potassium 105mg	**3%**	**9%**
Total Carbohydrate 24g	**8%**	**10%**
Dietary Fiber 3g	**12%**	**12%**
Sugars 4g		
Other Carbohydrate 17g		
Protein 3g		

Vitamin A	10%	15%
Vitamin C	10%	10%
Calcium	2%	15%
Iron	45%	45%
Vitamin D	10%	25%
Thiamin	50%	50%
Riboflavin	50%	60%
Niacin	50%	50%
Vitamin B$_6$	50%	50%
Folic Acid	50%	50%
Vitamin B$_{12}$	50%	60%
Phosphorus	10%	20%
Magnesium	8%	10%
Zinc	50%	50%
Copper	4%	4%

* Amount in cereal. A serving of cereal plus skim milk provides 1g total fat, less than 5mg cholesterol, 270mg sodium, 310mg potassium, 30g total carbohydrate (10g sugars) and 7g protein.

** Percent Daily Values are based on a 2,000 calorie diet. Your daily values may be higher or lower depending on your calorie needs:

		Calories	2,000	2,500
Total Fat	Less than		65g	80g
Sat Fat	Less than		20g	25g
Cholesterol	Less than		300mg	300mg
Sodium	Less than		2,400mg	2,400mg
Potassium			3,500mg	3,500mg
Total Carbohydrate			300g	375g
Dietary Fiber			25g	30g

Breaking It Out

The next section breaks down where the food's calories are coming from.

It also gives the percent daily values for each nutrient. (A percent is a part of a whole. Fifty percent equals one-half. Twenty-five percent equals one-fourth.) People are supposed to eat a certain amount of each nutrient every day. The percent daily value column tells you how much of that amount is in a serving.

	% Daily Value**	
Total Fat 1g*	1%	2%
Saturated Fat 0g	0%	0%
Trans Fat 0g		
Polyunsaturated Fat 0g		
Monounsaturated Fat 0g		
Cholesterol 0mg	0%	1%
Sodium 210mg	9%	11%
Potassium 105mg	3%	9%
Total Carbohydrate 24g	8%	10%
Dietary Fiber 3g	12%	12%
Sugars 4g		
Other Carbohydrate 17g		
Protein 3g		
Vitamin A	10%	15%
Vitamin C	10%	10%
Calcium	2%	15%
Iron	45%	45%
Vitamin D	10%	25%
Thiamin	50%	50%
Riboflavin	50%	60%
Niacin	50%	50%
Vitamin B_6	50%	50%
Folic Acid	50%	50%
Vitamin B_{12}	50%	60%
Phosphorus	10%	20%
Magnesium	8%	10%
Zinc	50%	50%
Copper	4%	4%

First on the list is fat. You know that not all fats are created equal. It's saturated and trans fats that you have to watch out for. Foods with low saturated fat are good choices. Even better are foods with no saturated fat. In the trans fats columns, it's always best to look for a zero.

Cholesterol comes later on the list. Here's another column where you want to see low numbers. Low-cholesterol foods are good for your heart.

Further down are carbohydrates. You can see how many of the carbs come from fiber and how many come from sugar. It's OK to eat some carbs from fiber and some carbs from sugar. But it's a good idea to avoid high-carb foods made of refined sugar. (Refined sugar is the white sugar found in foods such as cakes, cookies, and candies.)

Lower on the list is protein. As you'll remember, protein is important for building bones and muscles. It's smart to look for foods that contain protein.

Finally, the label lists the vitamins and minerals that the food provides. Foods with plenty of vitamins and minerals help you get the nutrients you need. Try to look for vitamin- and mineral-rich foods.

Percent daily values are based on the amount of nutrients that most adults need. But kids might need different amounts. How active you are also determines how many nutrients you need.

The Big Picture

The nutrition facts panel is a good tool for choosing foods. But it's important to see the big picture. You need to find healthful foods you like. Don't worry about trying to get your grams and percentages to add up exactly. Just knowing what's in your food is a big step toward eating better. *When you're aware of what you're putting in your body, you're more likely to make smart choices.*

Add the Calories

You can add up the calories in a serving of food without even looking at the total calories. Multiply the grams of carbs and protein by four. Then multiply the grams of fat by nine. Add these two numbers together. You should get the total calories. (Sometimes there are small differences because of ingredients such as sweeteners and fiber. But the numbers should be close.)

carbs + protein x 4 =
fat x 9 =

Pay Attention to Sodium

The mineral sodium can play a big part in your health. Your body needs some sodium to work properly. But too much sodium can be hard on the kidneys. And it can raise your blood pressure. That can lead to serious problems like heart attacks and strokes. Limiting the amount of salt you use is a good way to help control your sodium.

Chapter 4

THE BENEFITS OF Nutrition

Are you a person who *"lives to eat"* or someone who *"eats to live"*?

Do you see food as a treat that you look forward to and enjoy? Or do you see it as a source of energy, something that allows you to be healthy and do other things in life?

Most people see food both ways. They know they need to fuel their bodies with healthful foods. But they also enjoy eating. They like to gather with family around the dinner table. They have fun going out to eat with friends. For most people, food is never going to be just fuel. Food is a big part of your life. And you have no reason not to enjoy it.

The trick to good nutrition is finding healthful foods that you like. You need a careful balance and variety of foods to stay healthy. You can't eat pizza and burgers every day. But you can't eat only salads and healthful soy products either. Finding healthful foods that taste good is the key to maintaining good nutrition. *A good diet along with exercise allows you to be as healthy as you can be.*

Weight Problems

Maintaining a healthful weight is an issue for millions of people. Obesity has become a serious problem. Not all cases of obesity are related to diet. But most of them are.

People who become obese eat more calories than they can use, or burn up. The body turns those extra calories into fat. Over time, the calories can add up and people gain weight. The extra weight can cause serious health problems.

Heart disease is one health problem linked to obesity. When a body is carrying a lot of extra weight, the heart has to work harder to pump blood. In addition, obesity and high cholesterol often go hand in hand. High levels of bad cholesterol can often lead to heart attacks. Other problems obesity can cause are **knee, hip, and back pain**; **high blood pressure**; and **sleep disorders**.

Malnutrition is another condition caused by eating the wrong amount of calories or the wrong foods. Malnutrition is a lack of proper nutrients. It can result from a diet that's too low in calories. It can also result from a diet that lacks variety.

The effects of malnutrition vary. But in general, without enough nutrients, the body's organs begin to fail. The bones become brittle. They break easily. The muscles become weak. The mind can become clouded. Ultimately, malnutrition can lead to death.

Some eating disorders are similar to malnutrition. Eating disorders are conditions that interfere with a person's normal eating patterns. For example, a person with an eating disorder may severely limit what he or she eats. He or she may skip meals or refuse to eat foods containing fat.

People with eating disorders may have the same health issues as people with malnutrition. Without the nutrients it needs, the body just doesn't work properly.

Anorexia and Bulimia

The two most common eating disorders are anorexia and bulimia. Anorexia is when a person stops eating or eats very little in order to lose weight. People with anorexia may look extremely thin. But the condition prevents them from seeing themselves that way.

People with bulimia follow a behavior pattern called binge and purge. That means they may overdo the amount of calories they take in (binge) by eating a lot of food at once. Then they may get rid of all the calories (purge) by forcing themselves to throw up. Bulimics also might purge calories by overdoing physical activity. They might exercise until they're exhausted to keep from gaining weight.

Both anorexia and bulimia are very dangerous. Left untreated, they can even be deadly.

Improper Nutrition and Illness

Improper nutrition can do many things to your body. Missing even just one key nutrient can harm your health. For example, an illness called scurvy results from a lack of vitamin C. Sailors used

to come down with scurvy centuries ago. It's really just a form of malnutrition. But most sailors got plenty of calories. They ate fish, grains, bread, and more. The one thing they couldn't get at sea was fresh fruits and vegetables. Because of this, they had no vitamin C in their diets.

Over time, the sailors grew pale. They got bruises on their skin. Their gums started bleeding. Their energy levels dipped. Many of them became depressed. If they didn't find a way to get some vitamin C, they eventually died. Scurvy is rare in modern times. But it shows how the lack of just one key nutrient can affect your body.

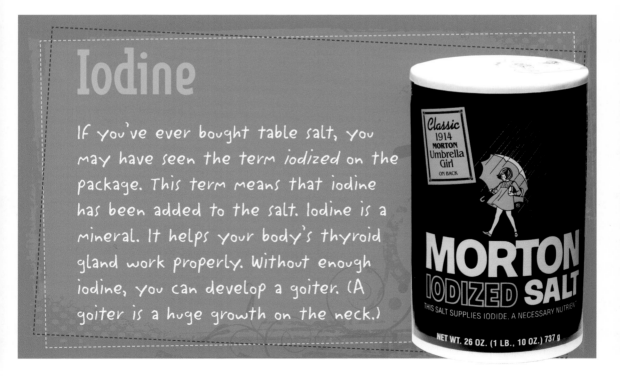

Iodine

If you've ever bought table salt, you may have seen the term *iodized* on the package. This term means that iodine has been added to the salt. Iodine is a mineral. It helps your body's thyroid gland work properly. Without enough iodine, you can develop a goiter. (A goiter is a huge growth on the neck.)

A Healthy Body

Good nutrition also affects your energy level. If you're eating right, your body will be less prone to injury and illness. You'll be better able to fight off colds and the flu. With good nutrition, you'll perform better in sports or other physical activities. You'll also do better in the classroom.

Keeping your body in the best possible shape is really pretty simple. Just eat a balanced diet and get exercise. If you do, you'll feel better and look better. You'll probably even live longer. When you look at it that way, there's really no reason not to strive for a healthful diet.

Vitamin Deficiencies

The chart below lists a few important vitamins and minerals and what happens if your body isn't getting enough of them.

VITAMIN/MINERAL	SOURCES	RESULT OF DEFICIENCY
vitamin A	fruits, leafy veggies	blindness
vitamin C	citrus fruits, veggies	scurvy
vitamin D	sunlight, eggs, milk*	rickets (malformed bones)
thiamine (B$_1$)	meat, grains	muscle weakness, paralysis
niacin (B$_3$)	milk, meat, grains	skin disorders, mental illness
potassium	meat, fruit	heart problems, nerve problems
calcium	milk, cheese, veggies	osteoporosis (weak bones)
iron	meat, grains, beans	anemia (low red-blood cell count, which leads to fatigue—or extreme tiredness)

*Vitamin D is added to milk to make it even more nutritious.

Chapter 5

MORE ABOUT Diets

As you'll remember from chapter 1, a diet is simply the combination of all the foods that you eat.

This means that everyone's on a diet!

If your diet is balanced and you're in good health, there's no need to change your eating habits. **The only diet you need is a healthful one.**

But special weight-loss diets seem to be everywhere. How do they work? Well, diets work by reducing the amount of calories a person eats. Exercise is also an important part of any diet plan. That's because exercise burns calories. People lose weight when they burn more calories than they take in.

The Mathematics of Dieting

It all boils down to simple math. If you eat 2,000 calories per day and burn off 2,500 calories, your body has to burn fat to get that extra energy. If you do this over weeks or months, your body will begin to have less and less fat.

On the other hand, if you eat the same number of calories but burn off only 1,500 through activity, your body will store the extra energy as fat. Over time, you will gain weight. This example shows that maintaining a healthful weight isn't just about nutrition. It's also about activity. The two go hand in hand.

NUTRITION

ACTIVITY

If you burn 3,500 more calories than you take in, you'll lose 1 pound (0.5 kilograms) of fat.

Low-fat Diets

One way people cut back on calories is by going on low-fat diets. Low-fat diets have been popular for decades. The idea seems simple. If you eat less fat, you'll have less fat in your body. But it's not as simple as it sounds. Fat in your diet doesn't necessarily become fat in your body. It's the calories in fat that can lead to weight gain. **Remember: a gram of fat has more than twice the calories as a gram of carbs or protein.** So if cutting down on fat helps a dieter cut back on calories, then a low-fat diet can help with weight loss. It's just important not to leave out the healthful unsaturated fats that the body needs.

Did You Know?

Some people go on diets to gain weight. Wrestlers, boxers, football players, and other athletes sometimes eat special foods in hopes of adding pounds. Weight-gain diets often contain lots of protein.

Low-Carb Diets

Low-carb diets have been popular in recent years. Low-carb diets work by cutting carbs. Like low-fat diets, low-carb diets paired with exercise can work. But in the end, what really makes the difference is the cut in calories, not in carbs.

One possible danger with low-carb diets is that they encourage people to eat lots of meat, eggs, and cheese. These foods are important. But they represent only a couple of food groups. And these food groups often contain fat. Getting too much of these foods could be dangerous. Many experts fear that low-carb diets strain the kidneys. They can raise cholesterol and put people at risk for heart disease too. Some low-carb diets also discourage eating enough fruits and vegetables. **People on these diets have to be sure their bodies are getting all the nutrients they need.**

Points Diets

Points diets are another popular option. These diets are very straightforward. Each food is worth a certain number of points. Dieters count up points for every food they eat. The goal is to hit a target number of points each day.

In the end, points diets boil down to counting calories. As long as a points diet is balanced and includes exercise, it can be useful. Some dieters like the structure points diets provide.

Certain diets have nothing to do with gaining or losing weight. Some vegetarians, for example, avoid meat because they don't believe in using animals as food.

Choose Wisely

Remember: you should never go on a special diet without first talking to a doctor. And in any diet, balance is important. Weight loss at the cost of good nutrition isn't going to help you.

You have to consider your overall health in any diet you choose. Whether you want to lose a few pounds or just want to live a healthier life, pairing good food choices with exercise is the way to go. *If you give your body the fuel it needs, you'll be on your way to a healthier, happier life.*

Crash Diets

Many people go too far when they start a diet. They drastically cut their calories in hopes of quick weight loss. This is a dangerous way of dieting. Many side effects can occur. Here are just a few of them:

fatigue

rashes

loss of muscle tone

sinus problems

fainting

depression

Chapter 6

MAKING Healthful Choices

Nutrition isn't just about the food you eat.

It's also about choosing to live a healthful, active life.

Nutrition is about taking charge of your body. It's about making healthful choices so you can look and feel your best.

Choose Exercise

One of the best things you can do for your health is to pair good nutrition with an active lifestyle. Some people get their exercise by running or by going to a gym. Treadmills, stair-climbing machines, and rowing machines are great ways to get a workout. But there are lots of other ways to burn off the calories you eat. Even simple choices can have an impact on your physical fitness. On a nice day, do you walk to a friend's house or ask for a ride? Do you stay inside and surf the Internet, or do you go out to find a basketball game to join? Exercise doesn't have to happen in a gym. Everyday activities can often give your body the workout it needs.

Whatever activities you choose, you should get at least one hour of physical activity each day. And you should try not to spend more than one hour per day in front of a computer or TV screen. (Not even to play your favorite video game!) It may be tempting to watch TV instead of doing something active. But exercise is good for both your body and your mind. It will help you feel better, look better, and sleep better.

More than 60 percent of all deaths in the United States are caused by cardiovascular diseases (diseases of the heart or blood vessels). Many of these result from poor physical fitness.

Burning Calories

Below is a chart of common activities and the number of calories each activity takes. This chart shows how many calories a 100-pound (45-kg) person can burn doing these activities. If you weigh less, you'll burn fewer calories. If you weigh more, you'll burn more.

Activity	Miles or Kilometers per Hour	Calories Burned per Hour
walking	3, or 5	225
jogging	5.5, or 9	500
running	10, or 16	900
bicycling	12, or 19	290
jumping rope		525
playing tennis		280
cross-country skiing		500

Choose Water

One of the easiest ways to get off track with your nutrition is by drinking lots of soda. It's easy to grab a can of soda instead of pouring a glass of water. But water is the best choice when it comes to quenching thirst. Diet and regular soda lack nutrients. They also contain acid. Acid can be hard on your teeth. And a regular soda has 100 calories or more. Worse still, almost all of them are from simple carbohydrates. (These carbs give you lots of energy at first—but they soon leave you feeling hungry and sluggish.) Water, on the other hand, *has no calories at all!*

The 100 or so calories in a soda may not sound like a lot. But they really add up. Think of it this way. If you drink one can of regular soda every day for a year, you're getting 36,500 calories or more. If you don't do extra activity to burn off those calories, they'll add up to about 15 pounds (6 kg) in fat. If you drink two cans of soda a day, those numbers double. *When you think about it that way, doesn't water sound like the smarter choice?*

Eight Glasses a Day?

You may have heard that you need to drink eight glasses of water a day. There's no doubt that water is good for you. But you probably don't really need eight glasses every day. Instead, choose a glass of water whenever you're thirsty. It's the most hydrating thing you can drink. And remember: You'll need plenty of water when you're physically active—or when temperatures rise in the summer.

Choose to Stick to the Plan

There are some simple choices you can make to help you maintain a healthful diet. If you're having a hard time sticking to the number of daily calories the USDA recommends for you, the following ideas can help.

1 **Eat a balanced breakfast.**
Breakfast is truly the most important meal of the day. Unfortunately, it's also the easiest meal to skip. Mornings can be busy. It can seem hard to slow down long enough to eat a healthful breakfast. But if you skip breakfast, you may be tempted to overeat throughout the rest of the day. You also may be tired and sluggish. That can reduce the amount of physical activity you get during the day.

2 **Go with smaller portions.** Most people tend to clear their plates regardless of how much food is on them. Often people force themselves to finish meals—even when they're full. Try dishing up portions that are just a bit smaller than what you're used to. Odds are, when you clean your plate, you won't even miss those last few bites. And if you're full and there's still a little food on your plate, don't feel like you have to finish. Your body is telling you that it has had enough.

3 **Eat slowly.** Your stomach needs time to tell you that it's full. The message takes as long as twenty minutes to get to your brain. So if you're eating quickly, you may be eating a lot more than your body really needs. Take it slow. If you're eating with others, try to carry on a conversation between bites. As a general rule, the slower you eat, the less you'll eat.

4 **Don't eat in front of the TV.** Or the computer. Instead, sit at a table while you eat. It'll make your meals more enjoyable. It'll also make you more aware of what—and how much—you are putting into your mouth.

5 **Keep busy.** A lot of people find themselves eating when they're bored. The best way to avoid this pitfall is to keep busy. Hang out with friends. Start a new hobby. Take a walk or ride a bike. If you find yourself headed to the kitchen just because you're bored, try to think of something else you could be doing. If you choose something that will keep you physically active, you're doing twice as much good.

Good nutrition is all about making SMART DECISIONS.

For many of us, bad habits are hard to break. People who are used to drinking three or four sodas a day have a hard time changing that behavior. But it's an important change to make. If you've got the choice of cookies or an apple as an after-school snack, it can be hard to resist the cookies. And sometimes, it's OK to make that choice. But to take charge of your own body, it's important to make the smart choice more often than not.

If YOU DO, your body will thank you for it.

Quiz

Now that you've read all about nutrition, try this fun quiz to see how much you know. Please record your answers on a separate sheet of paper. (Answers appear near the bottom of page 57.)

1. **Which meal would provide you with foods from all five of MyPyramid's major food groups?**

   a. A salad with lettuce, cheese, ham, and nuts

   b. An apple, a glass of milk, and a turkey-and-tomato sandwich on whole-wheat bread

   c. Whole-grain pasta with tomato sauce and cheese

   d. Cotton candy, pickles, and a root beer float

2. **Which nutrient contains the most calories per gram?**

   a. Fat

   b. Chocolate

   c. Carbohydrates

   d. Protein

3. **Which mineral helps oxygen get from your blood to your cells?**

   a. Potassium

   b. Calcium

   c. Bug guts

   d. Iron

4. **Which is the best strategy for losing weight?**

   a. Burn more calories than you take in

   b. Take in more calories than you burn

   c. Wash every meal down with a giant bottle of soda

   d. Cut out all fat

5. **What are enzymes?**

   a. Nutrients

   b. Small green men from another planet

   c. Digestive chemicals

   d. Vitamins

6. **It can be a bad idea to skip breakfast because:**

   a. You may be tempted to overeat throughout the rest of the day.

   b. You'll miss out on the chance to throw cereal at your brother.

   c. You may end up feeling tired and sluggish.

   d. Both a and c

7. **According to MyPyramid, which food group should be a central part of most diets?**

   a. The grains group

   b. The meat and beans group

   c. The milk group

   d. The sugar and spice group

8. **If you burn more calories than you eat, how does your body get extra energy?**

   a. By doing jumping jacks

   b. By using dietary fiber

   c. By making extra protein

   d. By burning fat

9. **Which condition occurs when someone isn't getting enough nutrients?**

   a. Obesity

   b. The flu

   c. Malnutrition

   d. High cholesterol

10. **Which of the following would be the most healthful choice at a fast-food restaurant?**

    a. Two large baskets of breaded chicken strips and deep-fried potato wedges on the side

    b. A grilled chicken salad

    c. A burger with onion rings

    d. A fried fish sandwich and the gooiest ice cream sundae on the menu

1. b; 2. a; 3. d; 4. a; 5. c; 6. d; 7. a; 8. d; 9. c; 10. b

Answers

MY NUTRITION LOG
Do you eat a balanced diet? Here's a simple activity that will help you better understand what you're putting into your body.

Start by finding a notebook to write in. Next, choose a day to keep track of everything you eat and drink. Mark the date on the top of the first page of your notebook.

As you go through your day, write down everything you eat. If you have a sandwich with bread, ham, and cheese, write down each food item separately. With some foods, it may be difficult to separate the different parts. Use ingredients lists to do your best.

At the end of the day, look over your list. Next to each food, write down which food group it comes from. Don't forget to track sweets and oils as well as the major food groups.

Count up the totals for each food group. Was your diet balanced? Did you leave any food groups out? If so, where might you have added them? Think about some foods you like that fit into the food groups you might have missed. You may want to try fitting those foods into your diet tomorrow.

Try keeping a nutrition log on different days. Your eating habits on a school day might be very different from your habits on a weekend. Over time, you'll be able to notice patterns. Maybe you tend to eat lots of sweets after dinner. Or maybe you aren't getting a balanced breakfast. Just knowing what you're putting into your body can have a big impact on the choices you make.

Here's a sample nutrition log to help you get started with your own nutrition record keeping:

NUTRITION LOG

September 23
—a bowl of oatmeal (grains) topped with pecans (meat and beans) and banana slices (fruits), a glass of milk (milk)

—a spinach salad (vegetables) with tomatoes (vegetables) and an olive oil dressing (oils), a turkey sandwich (meat and beans) served on whole-grain bread (grains), two glasses of water

—a handful of almonds (meat and beans), an apple (fruits), a glass of water

—whole-wheat pasta (grains) with tomato sauce (vegetables) and grilled chicken (meat and beans), peas (vegetables), a slice of bread (grains) dipped in olive oil (oils), a glass of milk (milk), a slice of chocolate cake (sweets)

—cheese slices (milk) on whole-grain crackers (grains), grapes (fruits), a glass of water.

Glossary

amino acid: the basic building block of a cell

calorie: a measurement of the amount of energy a certain food gives you

carbohydrate: a nutrient found in sugars and starches

cholesterol: a waxy substance found in animal tissues and cells. There are two kinds of cholesterol: HDL (good cholesterol) and LDL (bad cholesterol).

diet: the combination of all the foods you eat

eating disorder: a condition that interferes with a person's normal eating patterns

enzyme: a digestive chemical

glucose: a sugar that your body uses for energy. Glucose is also known as blood sugar.

malnutrition: a lack of proper nutrients

MyPyramid: the U.S. Department of Agriculture's guide to healthful eating

nutrient: a healthful substance found in food

obesity: a condition in which a person's body carries a large amount of fat

protein: a nutrient made of amino acids. Protein helps build bones and muscles.

scurvy: an illness caused by a lack of vitamin C

vegetarian: a person who does not eat meat

Carr, Timothy P. *Discovering Nutrition*. Malden, MA: Blackwell, 2003.

Ditson, Mary, Caesar Pacifici, and Lee White. *The Teenage Human Body: Operator's Manual*. Eugene, OR: Northwest Media, 1998.

Nemours Foundation. *KidsHealth*. 2007. http://www.kidshealth.org (November 26, 2007).

Smolin, Lori A., and Mary B. Grosvenor. *Nutrition and Weight Management*. Philadelphia: Chelsea House, 2005.

USDA. *MyPyramid.gov*. N.d. http://www.mypyramid.gov/ (November 26, 2007).

Weil, Andrew. *Eating Well for Optimum Health: The Essential Guide to Food, Diet, and Nutrition*. New York: Knopf, 2000.

Willett, Walter C. *Eat, Drink, and Be Healthy: The Harvard Medical School Guide to Healthy Eating*. New York: Free Press, 2005.

Learn More about Nutrition

Ballard, Carol. *The Digestive System*. Chicago: Heinemann Library, 2003. This book provides an overview of the digestive system and its individual organs.

Bickerstaff, Linda. *Nutrition Sense: Counting Calories, Figuring Out Fats, and Eating Balanced Meals*. New York: Rosen, 2005. Bickerstaff offers a simple guide to nutrition and explains how to apply it to a daily diet.

Doeden, Matt. *Stay Fit!: How You Can Get in Shape*. Minneapolis: Lerner Publications Company, 2009. Learn how physical activity and good nutrition work hand in hand to help you stay healthy and happy.

Gray, Shirley Wimbish. *Eating for Good Health*. Chanhassen, MN: Child's World, 2004. Gray tells all about how to care for your body by eating healthful foods.

It's My Life
http://pbskids.org/itsmylife
This website features useful information on a variety of health-related issues. A special section on the body introduces facts about nutrition and eating habits.

KidsHealth
http://www.kidshealth.org/kid
This site contains a wealth of information to help kids better understand how to lead a healthful lifestyle.

MyPyramid
http://www.mypyramid.gov
Visit this page to learn more about MyPyramid—the USDA's guide to healthful eating.

Petrie, Kristin. *A Passion for Proteins*. Edina, MN: Abdo, 2004. Petrie offers a simple introduction to protein, a nutrient that's essential to good health.

Schwager, Tina, and Michele Schuerger. *The Right Moves to Getting Fit & Feeling Great*. Minneapolis: Free Spirit, 1998. This guide aimed at girls provides tips on fitness, healthful eating, and maintaining a good self-image.

Index

Photo/Illustration Acknowledgments

The images in this book are used with the permission of: © Kuttig - People/Alamy, p. 4; Image Source Royalty Free Images, p. 6; © image100 Ltd./CORBIS, p. 8 (bottom); USDA, p. 8 (top); © Comstock Images, pp. 9 (top), 10 (bottom), 18 (top), 19, 21, 37 (top), 56; © Photodisc/Getty Images, pp. 9 (bottom), 23 (background); ©Todd Strand/Independent Picture Service, pp. 10 (top), 27, 28, 31, 37 (bottom); © Dorling Kindersley/Getty Images, p. 11 (top); © iStockphoto.com/Thomas Pullicino, p. 11 (center); © Juan Silva/Photographer's Choice/Getty Images, p. 13 (top); © Nana Twumasi/Independent Picture Service, p. 13 (bottom); © Mary Kate Denny/Stone/Getty Images, p. 14; © Xenia Demetriou-xeniaphotos.com/ Alamy, p. 16; © Bubbles Photolibrary/Alamy, p. 17 (top); © Peter Cade/ Stone/Getty Images, p. 17 (bottom); © Royalty-Free/CORBIS, p. 18 (bottom); Agricultural Research Service, USDA, p. 22; © Alistair Berg/ Taxi/Getty Images, p. 25; © Jenny Acheson/Riser/Getty Images, p. 26; © age fotostock/SuperStock, pp. 32, 35, 44, 50, 57; © Ryan McVay/ Photodisc/Getty Images, p. 33; © Ace Stock Limited/Alamy, p. 40; © Stockbyte/Getty Images, p. 41; © iStockphoto.com/Len Kaltman, p. 43; © Peter Chadwick/Dorling Kindersley/Getty Images, p. 45; © Kevin Dodge/CORBIS, p. 46; © Larry Prosor/SuperStock, p. 48; © iStockphoto.com/ Alberto Pomares, p. 49; © iStockphoto.com/Bruce Shippee, p. 52; © Digital Vision/Getty Images, p. 53.

Front Cover: © Asia Images Group/AsiaPix/Getty Images.

About the Author

Matt Doeden is a freelance author and editor living in Minnesota. He's written and edited hundreds of children's books on topics ranging from genetic engineering to rock climbing to monster trucks.